Forever Yours Marie-Lou

a play by

Michel Tremblay

translated by John Van Burek & Bill Glassco

P9-AQW-277

Copyright © 1971 Leméac Éditeur Inc.
Translation copyright © 1990 John Van Burek and Bill Glassco

Published with assistance from the Canada Council.

Talonbooks
P.O. Box 2076, Vancouver, British Columbia, Canada V6B 3S3
www.talonbooks.com

Typeset in New Baskerville and printed and bound in Canada. Printed on 100% post-consumer recycled paper.

Sixth Revised Printing: December 2010

No part of this book, covered by the copyright hereon, may be reproduced or used in any form or by any means—graphic, electronic or mechanical—without prior permission of the publisher, except for excerpts in a review. Any request for photocopying of any part of this book shall be directed in writing to Access Copyright (The Canadian Copyright Licensing Agency), 1 Yonge Street, Suite 800, Toronto, Ontario, Canada M5E 1E5; Tel.: (416) 868-1620; Fax: (416) 868-1621.

Rights to produce *Forever Yours, Marie-Lou*, in whole or in part, in any medium by any group, amateur or professional, are retained by the author. Interested persons are requested to apply to his agent: John C. Goodwin and Associates, 839 Sherbrooke est, Suite 2, Montréal, Québec H2L 1K6; Tel.: (514) 598-5252; www.agencegoodwin.com.

À Toi, pour toujours, ta Marie-Lou was first published by Leméac Éditeur Inc., Montréal, Québec. Published by arrangement with Leméac Éditeur Inc.

Canadian Cataloguing in Publication Data

Tremblay, Michel, 1942–
    [À Toi, pour toujours, ta Marie-Lou. English]
    Forever yours, Marie-Lou

    A play.
    Translation of: À toi, pour toujours, ta Marie-Lou.
    ISBN 0-88922-349-1

    I. Title. II. Title: À toi, pour toujours, ta Marie-Lou.
    English.
PS8539.R47A7913   C842'.54   C94-910357-8
PQ3919.2.T73A7913 1994

ISBN-13: 978-0-88922-349-3

A Toi, Pour Toujours, Ta Marie-Lou was first performed at Théâtre de Quat'Sous in Montréal, Québec, on April 29, 1971, with the following cast:

Marie-Louise	Hélène Loiselle
Léopold	Lionel Villeneuve
Carmen	Luce Guilbeault
Manon	Rita Lafontaine

Directed by André Brassard

Forever Yours, Marie-Lou was first performed in English at Tarragon Theatre in Toronto, Ontario, on November 4, 1972, with the following cast:

Marie-Louise	Patricia Hamilton
Léopold	George Sperdakos
Carmen	June Keevil
Manon	Toby Tarnow

Directed by Bill Glassco

Forever Yours, Marie-Lou was first performed in this new English translation at the Stratford Festival in Stratford, Ontario, on June 8, 1990, with the following cast:

Marie-Louise	Susan Wright
Léopold	Shaun Austin-Olsen
Carmen	Julia Winder
Manon	Marti Maraden

Directed by Lorne Kennedy
Designed by Brian Perchaluk
Music by Keith Thomas
Lighting designed by Kevin Fraser

The set is divided into three parts: the centre-backstage is a very clean, but very dark kitchen decorated exclusively with pious images, statues, candles, etc.; on the left is a living room with a sofa, a television, and a small table; on the right, a tavern table with three chairs. The kitchen should be as realistic as possible, but the other parts of the set may be incomplete or even merely suggested.

In the back, above the three parts of the set hangs a huge photograph, representing four young girls in the '40s, beaming at the camera. At the bottom of the photograph, one can read: "Forever Yours, Marie-Lou." Above the head of one of the girls a child has made a cross and written: "Maman, age 18."

The double action of the play takes place in the kitchen, but I wanted to "plant" MARIE-LOUISE and LEOPOLD in their favourite spots: MARIE-LOUISE is sitting in front of her television, knitting, and LEOPOLD is sitting in the tavern in front of a half dozen beers. As for MANON and CARMEN, they are actually sitting in the kitchen.

The two conversations (MARIE-LOUISE-LEOPOLD, CARMEN-MANON) take place ten years apart but they intermingle throughout the play. Thus it is very important that the spectator feel that MARIE-LOUISE and LEOPOLD are in the early 1960s while CARMEN and MANON are in the 1970s. It is also important (perhaps through a change in lighting) that the audience realize when CARMEN and MANON become characters in the past, in other words, girls fifteen or sixteen years of age.

MARIE-LOUISE and LEOPOLD never move, never look at one another. They stare straight ahead. They will only look at one another during the last two lines of the play.

§

MARIE-LOUISE
Tomorrow ...

CARMEN
Wow ...

LEOPOLD
Yeah ...

MANON
Still ...

MARIE-LOUISE
Tomorrow ...

CARMEN
Wow ...

LEOPOLD
Yeah ...

MANON
Still ...

Silence.

MARIE-LOUISE
Tomorrow we gotta ...

CARMEN
Wow, it's already ...

LEOPOLD
Yeah, I know ...

MANON
Still, it feels ...

Silence.

MARIE-LOUISE
> Tomorrow we gotta eat at my mother's ...

CARMEN
> Wow, it's already ten years ...

LEOPOLD
> Yeah, I know ... It's a pain in the ass.

MANON
> Still, it feels like yesterday ...

MARIE-LOUISE
> You think I feel like it?

CARMEN
> Ten years ...

LEOPOLD
> If you don't want to go either, we'll stay here, for Christ sake.

MANON
> Ten years ...

MARIE-LOUISE
> You want more coffee, Léopold?

> *Silence.*

> You want more coffee, Léopold?

> *Silence.*

> Do you want more coffee, Léopold?

CARMEN
> Ten Years!

LEOPOLD
>No, but you can make me more toast.

MANON
>Ten years ...

LEOPOLD
>Two pieces.

MARIE-LOUISE
>You ought to be careful ... You eat too much bread
>... The doctor ...

CARMEN
>A lot of water under the bridge ...

LEOPOLD
>Screw the doctor, make me more toast ...

MANON
>No ...

LEOPOLD
>And don't burn them.

MANON
>Everything's stayed the same ...

LEOPOLD
>I want them light.

CARMEN
>Maybe for you, ...

LEOPOLD
>Nice and light ...

CARMEN
        For me, everything's changed ...

LEOPOLD
        Forget it ... I'll do it myself.

MARIE-LOUISE
        I can make your toast. I'm not sick.

CARMEN
        Everything's changed.

MARIE-LOUISE
        I'm not sick!

MANON
        If you think walking out the door changed
        everything ...

CARMEN
        I don't think it, Manon, I did it.

LEOPOLD
        I think I will have a coffee ...

MANON
        And look what you've become!

LEOPOLD
        If it's not cold.

MANON
        Look what you've become! You belong in a circus.

LEOPOLD
        The last cup wasn't very hot.

MANON
        I'd be ashamed to be seen on the street like that.

8

MARIE-LOUISE
Why didn't you stay in bed?

MANON
Would you mind telling me ...

MARIE-LOUISE
It's Saturday ...

MANON
... Where you dug up that ridiculous outfit?

CARMEN
When you decide to change, Manon, you change everything. Everything.

LEOPOLD
You woke me up when you got out of bed.

CARMEN
In ten years I've become another woman.

MARIE-LOUISE
Ah, ... I didn't mean to ... I tried to be quiet.

MANON
Ten years ...

LEOPOLD
You woke me up when you ran out of the room, Marie-Louise.

MANON
Boy ...

LEOPOLD
I heard your concert in the bathroom, every bloody note.

MANON
>It's unbelievable ...

LEOPOLD
>Don't worry, you left the door open just enough so everybody could hear. And now I suppose you're gonna play the martyr all weekend.

MARIE-LOUISE
>I didn't have time to close the door. I had to run. I didn't have time.

LEOPOLD
>Come on, you must have known you were gonna be sick. You could have gotten up sooner.

MANON
>It's like a long grey ribbon behind me ... All the same ...

CARMEN
>Because you wanted it that way ... If you'd tried to get out, even a bit ...

LEOPOLD
>We'll hear about it all weekend ...

CARMEN
>But no ... You spend your life hung up on that one Saturday.

LEOPOLD
>It's the first thing you'll tell your mother tomorrow.

CARMEN
>You sit here in the kitchen, like a prisoner, and you think about them.

LEOPOLD

Your eyes in the bean grease to get more pity.

CARMEN

For ten years you've done nothing but think about them.

LEOPOLD

That's your specialty, eh? The eyes in the bean grease.

CARMEN

Come on, get off your butt! Wake up! Get out of here!

MANON

The world's no better out there, Carmen.

CARMEN

Thanks a lot!

LEOPOLD

And then your mother will hand me one of her horseshit sermons.

MANON

I'm not about to dress up like a carnival queen to convince myself life is beautiful. Not after what happened.

LEOPOLD

I'm warning you, if your mother shoves one more sermon at me, I'll strangle her.

CARMEN

That was ten years ago, for God's sake. Forget it.

MANON
>So what if it's fifty years, what would that change?
Eh? What would it change?

MARIE-LOUISE
>I've a right to be sick, don't I?

MANON
>It's as if you've never given a moment's thought to
what he did. Don't you realize that ...

CARMEN
>That what?

MANON
>Nothing ... Forget it.

MARIE-LOUISE
>I've a right to be sick, too. So I made a little noise.
All you had to do was go back to sleep if you don't
care that I'm sick!

LEOPOLD
>Who says I don't care?

MARIE-LOUISE
>When you're sick, you don't even get up. You lie
there, sprawled all over the bed, moaning like a
foghorn, then you puke all over my sheets. My
mother's right to give you sermons. You're worse
than a kid.

CARMEN
>You still think you're smarter than me, don't you?

MANON
>No.

CARMEN
> Then why don't you answer? You know how I hate it, when you start to say something and don't finish!

LEOPOLD
> When it hits me, I can't do anything. It happens too fast ...

MARIE-LOUISE
> Liar.

MANON
> Why should I repeat what you already know?

MARIE-LOUISE
> You just love to feel sorry for yourself. You lie there in your slop and wait for me to clean you up. I didn't marry you to wipe up last night's beer, Léopold.

LEOPOLD
> You didn't marry me for much else either.

MANON
> I just wanted to talk about what Papa did ...

MARIE-LOUISE
> What's that supposed to mean?

CARMEN
> But we're not sure he did it, Manon.

LEOPOLD
> Nothing ... Forget it.

CARMEN
> There was never any proof.

MANON
    You need proof?

MARIE-LOUISE
    You know how I hate it when you start to say
    something and don't finish!

LEOPOLD
    Everything I have to say to you I've just said,
    Marie-Louise. You didn't marry me for much else.
    It's clear and that's that.

CARMEN
    You've got to stop thinking about that, Manon. You
    imagine things that didn't happen.

MANON
    Didn't happen!

CARMEN
    Not the way you see it.

MANON
    You don't believe that's what happened, eh?

CARMEN
    No.

MANON
    Liar! You know, like everyone else. And you all
    refuse to see what he did.

CARMEN
    Well, you only see what he didn't do ...

MANON
    You say don't think about it! How? We heard it with
    our own ears, Carmen. I can't stop thinking about

it. Even at work it's always on my mind. And when I
come back here ...

CARMEN

How many times have I told you to move? But you
don't want to move, do you? You don't want to
forget. Isn't that right?

LEOPOLD

Marie-Louise, your toast is burning!

MANON

Can't you get it through your head, nothing would
change if I moved!

LEOPOLD

Marie-Louise, your toast is burning!

MANON

I'd still hear them, Carmen. I can't get rid of their
voices.

LEOPOLD

Marie-Louise, the toast! Son-of-a-bitch, you do it on
purpose.

CARMEN

It's true, you're a lot like him.

MANON

Carmen!

MARIE-LOUISE

Will you keep your voice down! You want the whole
neighbourhood to hear?

CARMEN

Sorry ... That's not what I meant. It's just that
sometimes you're on the moon, like he was ...

MARIE-LOUISE
And you'll wake up the kids again.

The lights change.

And you'll wake up the kids again.

MANON
Carmen did you hear that? They're fighting again.

CARMEN
No, no, they're not fighting ... They're just arguing
...

MANON
It always starts like that, but it ends up in a fight.

CARMEN
I tell you, they're not gonna fight ...

MANON
Go and see.

CARMEN
What?

MANON
Go see what they're doing ...

CARMEN
Are you crazy?

MANON
Go on, they won't hear you. I want to know what
they're saying.

LEOPOLD
The kids ...

CARMEN
     You don't need to know what ...

MANON
     I want to know what they say. I don't want him
     insulting her again.

LEOPOLD
     The kids aren't asleep ...

MANON
     Forget it, I'll go myself.

LEOPOLD
     The minute I got out of bed the kids were awake.

CARMEN
     Watch out, if you get caught ...

LEOPOLD
     Even if we whispered, they'd hear us. They always
     hear everything. They know everything. They're
     always behind some door, listening. I'll bet you a
     nickel that right now Carmen's hiding behind that
     kitchen door.

CARMEN
     Manon, get back here, you're gonna get caught.

MARIE-LOUISE
     You must be pretty sure of yourself to bet a nickel
     Léopold.

LEOPOLD
     You can go back to bed, Carmen. I'm not gonna kill
     your mother today. *The Police Gazette*'s headline
     won't be till next week. And don't bother to tiptoe,
     the floor squeaks anyway.

MANON

He knew I was there ...

CARMEN

I told you, stupid.

MANON

He thought it was you ...

CARMEN

Oh, great! Now who's gonna get yelled at?

MANON

Well, at least Roger didn't wake up ... Good thing ...

CARMEN

Get back into bed. It's none of our business.

LEOPOLD   *as the lights return to normal*

It's not kids we got, it's spies. Always sticking their noses where they don't belong. One of these days I'll smack the daylights out of them!

MARIE-LOUISE

One of these days ... Sure! Always later, eh, Léopold? Never right away, always later ... In a while ... Maybe tomorrow ... Or maybe next week ... In other words, never.

CARMEN

I'm convinced, if you'd take my advice ...

MANON

If I'd taken your advice I'd be like you today. No thanks.

CARMEN

Christ, will you let me finish!

MANON

And listen to your language.

CARMEN

I can never get two words in! I never asked you to be like me, you know!

LEOPOLD

Forget it, Marie-Louise, don't make more toast, I'll scrape these.

CARMEN

It was your idea that I wanted you to copy me. I don't want you to follow me! I just want you to get out of here ... and stop dreaming.

MANON

They're not dreams! You know they're not dreams. You're the one who's dreaming, Carmen. You live in a dream.

LEOPOLD

Any peanut butter left?

CARMEN

Well, if you think you live in the real world ...

MARIE-LOUISE

Yes ...

CARMEN

I prefer my dream.

MARIE-LOUISE

I mean, I bought a new jar ... The other was empty.

MANON

So, fine ... stay where you are ... I didn't ask you to wake up.

LEOPOLD

So ... Get it out ...

MARIE-LOUISE

They were out of Smoothy, Léopold, so ...

LEOPOLD

So you bought Crunchy again!

MARIE-LOUISE

They were out of Smoothy, goddamn it.

CARMEN

Christ, are you dumb!

MARIE-LOUISE

Are you gonna make a fuss over six cents?

MANON

That's right, I'm dumb. Everyone's always said so.

LEOPOLD

You're damn right I'm gonna make a fuss. If it's not peanut butter that costs more it's hamburger, sixty-nine a pound instead of forty-nine, if it's not hamburger, it's something else. And you always work it so when Tuesday comes, you ask me for more money.

MARIE-LOUISE

You don't give me enough.

LEOPOLD

I give you enough. Christ, I give you too much! You know what I make a week busting my ass behind that fucking machine just to feed all of you!

MARIE-LOUISE
>Sure I know, starvation wages, but that's no reason
to give up Crunchy peanut butter! Listen, you stingy
bastard, when you're busting your ass behind your
machine, just tell yourself that tomorrow you'll be
eating Crunchy peanut butter instead of Smoothy.
It's better than nothing.

CARMEN
>I'm gonna tell you something you won't like,
Manon. It's true you resemble him. You're just like
him.

MARIE-LOUISE
>Everytime I buy something a bit more expensive
you start foaming at the mouth. But that doesn't
stop you from eating it, does it? No! As soon as the
fit goes, so does the food. Right on to your plate.

CARMEN
>Well? ...

LEOPOLD
>It's normal for the man of the house to eat the
most. It's him who puts the food in your mouth! If I
wasn't here you'd starve to death.

MARIE-LOUISE
>If you weren't here, we wouldn't be either, and we'd
all be a lot better off.

CARMEN
>You know it's true, eh?

MARIE-LOUISE
>Do you want some more toast, Léopold? You wanna
finish up the bread? Then you can scream bloody

murder when I send Roger out to buy another loaf. When we were first married, you'd walk three miles, to save two cents on a tin of sardines! But now you're too fat, you're too lazy, so you run off at the mouth instead. Believe me, Léopold, I liked it better when you walked the three miles, Sure, I could have gone to Steinberg's to buy Smoothy, but I didn't feel like it. Sure, I could have saved six cents. So what? It's a long way to Steinberg's in the winter and I'm not about to freeze my feet for six cents.

CARMEN

That's why you hated him so much, eh? 'Cause you were just like him.

LEOPOLD

Now who's making a fuss? You want me to open the window so the neighbours can hear, then they can tell the whole world I don't feed you right ...

MARIE-LOUISE

Don't worry, you won't open the window, the house'd get cold and you'd have to turn up the heat ... That reminds me, we're almost out of oil. You gonna let us freeze to death like last year?

MANON

Once ... You and I were pretty small at the time ... I was maybe six or seven ...

MARIE-LOUISE

Don't pretend you didn't hear me, Léopold. We're out of oil.

LEOPOLD

So order some, for Chrissake! Buy Texaco!

MARIE-LOUISE
> As if we heat the house with Texaco! Idiot!

LEOPOLD
> We don't heat it with Crunchy peanut butter, either!

MANON
> We'd been invited to Mother's sister's place ... Ma
> tante Marguerite ... It was during the holiday, I
> think ... Everyone was there, the whole family ...
> There must have been fifty of us ... We didn't have a
> car in those days ... We went by streetcar ... You were
> holding on to Papa's hand, and I stayed close to
> Maman ... I'd try to walk like her ... smile like her ...
> I tried to give her my hand too, but she'd always let
> it go ... It's like she'd forget she was holding it and
> all of a sudden she'd drop it ... When we got to ma
> tante Marguerite's they were all over us ... You know
> how gushy they are on her side ... endless hugs and
> kisses ... Anyway, suddenly Grandpère was there,
> and with a big laugh he picked us both up in his
> arms. I was all excited because he was so tall and I
> was so high up ... He looked at you and he said,
> "You little bugger, you look exactly like your
> mother!" Everybody laughed ... When he looked at
> me I stopped laughing 'cause I knew what he was
> going to say. I started to struggle because I didn't
> want him to say it. "And you, Manon, the spitting
> image of your father." I could have scratched his
> eyes out! They talked about it for years after. I
> started hitting him in the face and screaming like a
> demon ... When they finally calmed me down they
> all began to say what a bad girl I was that I had no
> manners ... That I was uncontrollable ... Just like my
> father! Grandpère called me "Little Miss Poison."
> When we got back home I got the beating of my life

... He was drunk, and he was yelling, "So you don't want to look like me, eh, you don't want to look like me!" He knew ...

MARIE-LOUISE

Hey, you've eaten half the jar! All that peanut butter for two pieces of toast?

LEOPOLD

So, I paid for it.

MANON

And he's the only one who knew.

CARMEN

You think so?

MARIE-LOUISE

Let's see ... That's five jars of peanut butter for one loaf of bread ... Like they say on TV, boy, you sure don't know how to economize.

CARMEN

So what did it matter if you looked more like him than her?

MANON

He was a crazy bastard and I didn't want to look like him.

CARMEN

He was no worse than anyone else, Manon. Maybe just more fed up.

MARIE-LOUISE

Lift your elbow, Léopold, I need the tablecloth ... I'm gonna do the dishes ... Unless you want to finish off the peanut butter with a spoon, like you do at night.

LEOPOLD
>What? What did you say?

MARIE-LOUISE   *whispering*
>You think I don't know you give Roger a beating the other day ... For nothing.

>>*The lights change.*

>You think I don't know where all the strawberry jam went?

MANON
>You can't hear them now.

MARIE-LOUISE   *whispering*
>You know, when you get up at night, Léopold, you cough and fart all the way to the kitchen. The people downstairs must think the house is falling down.

MANON
>I'm worried, Carmen.

CARMEN
>You worry when they shout, you worry when they whisper ... Relax, for God's sake ...

MARIE-LOUISE
>Do you think we sleep like babies? You think we don't hear a thing? It's no sin to be hungry at night Léopold, especially when you're fat like you. Why won't you admit it?

LEOPOLD
>I told you the other day, I don't want to hear another word about that. Understand? Or I'll shove this Crunchy peanut butter right in your face!

CARMEN
     There, are you happy? He's yelling again.

MANON
     The bastard ...

MARIE-LOUISE   *whispering*
     To beat a kid for nothing when you know we're to
     blame!

LEOPOLD
     Look, goddamn it, I said the other day it was Roger
     who finished the strawberry jam. And it was him.
     Okay?

MARIE-LOUISE   *normal voice*
     Let go, you're hurting me. How do you know it was
     him, eh? Why couldn't it have been Manon, or
     Carmen? Why not me, eh? Why? It's 'cause Roger's
     the last, the smallest, 'cause he can't defend
     himself, he's easy to knock around, and you know
     he's terrified. You bastard! Coward! You yell and
     scream and wave your arms, but you're starting to
     get scared of your daughters 'cause they're not kids
     anymore. There's only one in the house you can
     push around now, and you jump on him with both
     feet. Well I have a little surprise for you Léopold. I
     have a little surprise. It won't be long before you
     have another one to beat the shit out of.

MANON
     Carmen, did you hear that?

MARIE-LOUISE
     Oh yes, he's in there all right! Doesn't that make
     you happy, my love? My pet? My sweetie-pie?
     Another one's on the way. Another gift from

Heaven. So go on, dance, whoop it up, shout it from the rooftops. Take me in your arms like they do in the movies and tell me "Darling, I'm so happy." Three months ago, when you came home drunk from your famous shop party, and threw yourself on me as if I were a whore on St-Laurent and you got me pregnant, Léopold. That's right, you got me pregnant! I told you, I pleaded with you to be careful, I fought to make you stop but you wouldn't listen, you were like a raging bull, you were calling me "bébé" as if I'd ever been your "bébé."

CARMEN

Manon, stay in bed. Stay out of this.

MARIE-LOUISE

It's like the three other times you've raped me. Léopold once again you've got me pregnant.

CARMEN

Come back here, you idiot, he'll kill you.

MARIE-LOUISE

But this time I'm too old to have a baby. I haven't the strength, Léopold. Do you hear me? I haven't the strength to have another.

>   *Long silence.*

>   *The lights turn to normal.*

You've nothing to say ... You've nothing to say. I suppose you don't believe me.

LEOPOLD

Of course I don't believe you. At your age? You're too old, Marie-Louise, you won't have any more

kids, you're past that. You're imagining things ... It's
normal for a woman your age to feel sick in the
morning ...

MANON
I was so ashamed I'd hug the walls when I walked
down the street.

MARIE-LOUISE
I've been to the doctor, Léopold ...

MANON
No matter how hard I tried to look like her ...

LEOPOLD   *trying to joke*
Hah! Women ...

MANON
... someone would always come along and burst my
balloon.

LEOPOLD
... You're all the same ...

CARMEN
There you said it yourself, you were in the clouds ...
Even when you were a kid ...

LEOPOLD
The minute your stomach's upset you get hysterical,
you think you're pregnant ...

CARMEN
I can remember too, Manon ... Whenever we played
house, you always had to be the mother. When I'd
get fed up and make you play father, all hell would
break loose. You'd kick and scream and threaten to
kill me ...

MANON
I never said that.

CARMEN
But you did, Manon. You see I'm not the only one who "forgets." I bet you even felt the same things he did when he got mad, eh? You even used to look at yourself in the mirror and say, "I'll kill you, you bastard! I'll kill you."

MARIE-LOUISE   *softly*
It was the doctor who told me, Léopold ...

CARMEN
And there was something else, wasn't there?

MANON
What do you mean, something else?

CARMEN
It wasn't just because you looked like him ... You had other reasons to hate him ...

MARIE-LOUISE
If you want proof I've been to the doctor, I'll show you the bill. It just arrived. You'll believe me when you see the amount, Léopold. It's a real doctor's bill, the kind you love to pay.

LEOPOLD
How long have you known?

MARIE-LOUISE
I've suspected it a while, but I've only known for two weeks.

MANON
When I was little there was nothing else ... I know

he made us all unhappy and I hated him ... But later ... Later there was something else ...

LEOPOLD
Why didn't you tell me before?

MARIE-LOUISE
I was afraid.

LEOPOLD
Why didn't you tell me before?

MARIE-LOUISE
Believe it or not, I was afraid of you, ... Because of Roger ... Remember what you wanted me to do when I was pregnant with Roger? Well, this time I decided I'd only tell you when it was too late.

LEOPOLD
A minute ago you said you weren't strong enough to have another baby ...

MANON
There was one other thing, ... And when I think about it, Carmen ...

MARIE-LOUISE   *making the sign of the cross*
It's too late. And, I'd never do that ... It's against nature.

CARMEN
When you think about what?

LEOPOLD
Sure, you'd rather see us sink deeper in the shit.

MARIE-LOUISE stops knitting.

Silence.

MARIE-LOUISE
>   You're right.

Silence.

CARMEN
>   You don't want to tell me?

MANON
>   I've already told you, but you've forgotten that too,
>   like you do everything else.

LEOPOLD
>   Where are we gonna put it? Eh? Where are we
>   gonna put it?

MARIE-LOUISE
>   We'll find a place ...

LEOPOLD
>   A place! What place? Where? Have you thought
>   about that? Eh? Where? Roger already sleeps on the
>   sofa and the girls bitch 'cause they're stuck in the
>   same room. So where are we gonna put it? Here, in
>   the kitchen? In the stove? In the fridge? In the sink?
>   In the garbage?

MARIE-LOUISE
>   We'll just have to put him in our room, Léopold.

LEOPOLD
>   In our room ... In our room! Are you out of your
>   mind? We're not Eskimos. There's no room in our
>   room. How we gonna get a cradle in that match-
>   box? It's no bigger than my mouth!

MARIE-LOUISE
    If it's as big as your mouth Léopold, we could open
    a school in there. We'll get rid of the TV, that's all.

LEOPOLD
    Oh, I get it. You'd do anything to get rid of that TV,
    won't you? Well, I got news for you, Marie. I told
    you before, if the television goes, I go too.
    Remember?

MARIE-LOUISE
    Sure, I remember. That was the night I put it in the
    living room ...

LEOPOLD
    And I'm telling you again, if that TV leaves the
    bedroom, I go with it. Okay?

MARIE-LOUISE
    That's fine ... I already told you, ... Move into the
    living room ... Roger can come and sleep with me.

LEOPOLD
    Whoever heard of a mother sleeping with her son?

MARIE-LOUISE
    Whoever heard of a husband who liked his TV more
    than his wife? Mind you ... we've all heard of that ...
    And it's true. For ten years now we've all come
    second ... Right after the Saturday night hockey ...
    The lot of us.

MANON
    Maybe I didn't tell you ...

MARIE-LOUISE
    The lot of us ...

MANON

He'd come home drunker than ever. It was already light out by the time he got in, and he started talking poetry to the moon ... He told the moon he didn't want it to go away and lots of crazy stuff like that. Maman tried to calm him down, but he just stood there in the dining room howling like a dog ...

CARMEN

That happened lots of times ...

MANON

Wait, there's more ... There was no way he'd go to bed, he wanted something to eat. So Maman made him some breakfast. When he finished he said he'd go to sleep. Maman said she'd make up the sofa in the living room, but no, he didn't want that. He insisted on sleeping in his own bed ... They yelled at each other for a while and then finally Maman gave in, as usual ... When they passed by our door she said "Don't you dare touch me ... I'm warning you." I didn't know what that meant yet, but still I was scared. He answered as he always did, "You're my wife, you obey me."

LEOPOLD

Whoever heard of a husband getting kicked out because of a TV?

MARIE-LOUISE

It's the sort of thing you don't say, Léopold. It's the sort of thing women keep secret because they're ashamed.

MANON

They finally got into their room. They weren't in

bed for two minutes when Maman started to yell at
him again. She called him every name in the book.
Then ... the blows started ...

LEOPOLD

Bullshit! I never heard of that.

MANON

I got out of bed ... I thought for sure he was going
to kill her ...

LEOPOLD

Liar. You're all liars! The TV stays where it is Marie-
Louise.

MANON

I crept down the hall and put my ear to the door ...

LEOPOLD

You can stick your kid wherever you like. I know
what, you can both sleep in the living room.
Roger'll come sleep with me. For a boy to sleep with
his father is normal. That won't make him a queer.

MANON

The door wasn't closed all the way and it swung
open a bit ... I really didn't want to look, you know
... I knew I shouldn't look in their room, ... But ... I
saw them, Carmen ... I saw them.

MARIE-LOUISE

I suppose it's normal for a man to kick his wife out
of bed after he's gotten her pregnant.

MANON

Maman was struggling, trying to fight him off ... He
was saying stuff, I couldn't hear what ... I could only

see them struggling ... I thought he was going to kill
her, and I started to cry ...

LEOPOLD

I'm not kicking you out, I'm just putting you in the
living room.

MARIE-LOUISE

No, no, I'm putting you in the living room. Anyway,
there's no question of our not sleeping in the same
bed. For the kids' sake.

LEOPOLD

Now wait just a minute. Have we done anything,
since we got married, that wasn't for the kids?

MARIE-LOUISE

We never had a choice. You got me pregnant right
away, Léopold.

MANON

They both turned around at the same time. I'll
never forget their faces, Carmen. They looked at
me for a few seconds then Maman let out this cry
and turned to the wall. Him, he just pulled up the
covers and said, "You can go back to bed, the show's
over."

LEOPOLD

That's right, it's always my fault ...

MARIE-LOUISE

That's right, it's always your fault ...

LEOPOLD

All the shit that lands on our heads, it's always my
fault ...

MARIE-LOUISE
	Yes ... always ...

LEOPOLD
	... Never yours ...

MARIE-LOUISE
	It's always your bloody fault. Always. No matter how
	hard I try to make things better, we always end up
	worse off than before.

LEOPOLD
	Small wonder if you try like you do with the
	Crunchy peanut butter! We could be up to our ears
	in shit ...

MARIE-LOUISE
	I put my foot in the shit when I said yes to you,
	Léopold ... But before I die in it I'm gonna say no a
	thousand times ...

MANON
	"Go back to bed, the show's over."

CARMEN
	That's all?

MANON
	If you'd seen them, Carmen ... If you'd seen them!
	They were so ugly!

CARMEN
	That's 'cause they didn't know how to do it.

MANON
	Carmen!

CARMEN

Well, it's true.

MANON

You'll never understand. I don't know why I ever told you ...

CARMEN

So I'd feel sorry for you, Manon, you know damn well. You think you're the only kid in the world who's walked in on her parents? Come off it!

LEOPOLD

Achhh, another kid! I don't believe it!

CARMEN

You make up horror stories, but you love it, don't you? Stop living in the past! I'll bet you anything you talk to the moon too. You sit here in your chair and you tell yourself stories about your wicked Papa who made you so miserable. Give me a break!

MANON

Well, didn't he make us miserable?

CARMEN

Sure, maybe he did, but life goes on! You mope around here rehashing everything he ever said and did ... and you expect the world to pity you. Well, you're not pitiable Manon ... not in the least!

LEOPOLD

Here we go again. Sleepless nights, bottles, diapers, the same fucking routine.

CARMEN

If you had half a brain in your head you'd stop feeling sorry for yourself and get rid of all this.

MANON

Like you, I suppose ...

CARMEN

Why not?

MANON

I have some respect.

CARMEN

It's not a question of respect. It's your life. You too, you've got to live your life.

MANON

How can I live my life with all these things in my head ...

CARMEN

Get them out of your head, that's all! How many times do I have to say it. This is unbelievable at your age! You've still got Mother's picture on the television. I bet you look at that more than the TV. I mean, put it in the garbage ... or in a drawer somewhere ... Okay, our father was a bit of a bastard, but he wasn't that bad. Don't make him such a monster. The way you talk, Mother was a saint.

MANON

She *was* a saint!

CARMEN

Manon, For God's sake! That's ridiculous!

MANON

And if she can hear you, she must be weeping ...

CARMEN

In Heaven, I suppose. I hope you're not going to

start on Heaven again this morning. Look, Manon, this whole thing's ridiculous. You are really crazy. For God's sake, our mother was not a martyr and our father was not the devil.

LEOPOLD

We're too old to start all that again ... Now get this, bitch, from now on, it's Smoothy peanut butter for you. You better watch every penny if you want that kid to be fed.

MANON   *low*

It marked me for life ... I know it marked me for life ... I don't care what you say ... There's nothing you can do to change it ... You didn't see them ...

MARIE-LOUISE

Your boss owes you a raise ... Tell him you need it ... Now you got another mouth to feed ...

CARMEN

Don't worry, I know it's not me who'll change a thing around here!

LEOPOLD

I'm not in a union shop. Raises don't just fall out of the sky.

CARMEN   *laughing*

I know what you need Manon ... A man.

MARIE-LOUISE

You're all too wimpy to get a union in there, so we all pay for it!

CARMEN

It's a man that you need. That'd calm you down a bit. If you'd try it for real instead of just thinking about what you saw ... Have you ever tried it, Manon?

MANON

Shut up! You don't known what you're talking about.

CARMEN

I don't know what I'm talking about?

MANON

You don't know what I mean ...

CARMEN

... I know what you mean ... Yes ... And you know something? It makes me sick.

MARIE-LOUISE

He's owed it to you for a year ... You'd shit your pants before you'd ask him ... He owes it to you, Léopold, he owes you money!

CARMEN

It makes me sick to see a girl like you, my own sister, ruin her life for nothing ...

MARIE-LOUISE

You scream bloody murder when I ask you for money but you're too dumb to ask your boss for the money he owes you. You'll always be a chicken.

CARMEN

For nothing ... It's all in your head.

MARIE-LOUISE

You're all alike. You shit on us 'cause we're beneath you and you let the ones on top shit all over you. Why take it out on us? Why don't you get rid of him?

CARMEN
>What the hell, maybe you're happy the way you are.
>I guess some people like being miserable.

LEOPOLD
>Twenty-seven years I've been working for that
>bastard ... and I'm only forty-five. It's almost funny
>to think at the age of eighteen you started working
>for a guy you hate and you're still there kissing his
>ass. There are still too many guys like me around.
>The kids today go to school, they won't make the
>same mistake. Jesus Christ! You spend your whole
>fucking life doing the same fucking thing at the
>same fucking machine. Your whole life! You're a
>specialist, my boy thank the good Lord! You're not
>part time, you've got a steady job. Every man's
>dream: a steady job? Is there anything worse in this
>world than a steady job. You become such a
>specialist in your steady job you become part of
>your fucking machine. It starts telling you what to
>do! You don't watch it, it watches you and as soon as
>you turn your back, pow ... Fucking bitch! You know
>her so well it's like you were born with her! Like she
>was your first toy, for Chrissake. When I got
>strapped to that fucking machine, I was hardly more
>than a kid. And I've still got twenty years to go! In
>twenty years there'll be nothing left of me. I'm
>already half dead. And in twenty years, my boy it's
>not you they'll retire, it's your machine! ... But I'm a
>specialist ... A specialist! I don't thank the good
>Lord one bit ... In fact the good Lord can shove it
>up his ass. Besides, you don't even work for yourself,
>it's all for your family! You sweat your balls off to
>earn a few lousy bucks and you hand the whole wad
>over to them. Your precious family! Another of the
>good Lord's great inventions! Four big mouths,
>gaping wide open and all ready to bite when you

41

walk in the door on Thursday night! And if you don't come straight home, 'cause maybe you feel like having a beer with your pals, watch out, they'll eat you alive! You walk in the door, in five minutes your pockets are picked clean and all you can do is fall into bed. And your family says it's 'cause you're drunk. Then they tell the whole world what a heartless bastard you are. That's right, a heartless bastard. Why hide it; you're a bastard.

CARMEN

If it hadn't been Papa you'd have found some other excuse to ruin your life. But he makes it easy for you, eh? Makes it easy to hate every man you meet. "My father was a bastard, so you're all bastards." Easy, eh? Gives you a clear conscience. Once, when we were little and we talked to one another, I asked you what you'd be when you grew up. Do you remember what you said? "When I grow up I want to be real sad and die like a martyr."

MANON

I feel whoozy again ...

LEOPOLD

Cut the crap!

CARMEN

If I'd known you meant it, I'd have strangled you on the spot.

MARIE-LOUISE

I'm going to have a baby Léopold! For the next six months I'll be sick to my stomach.

LEOPOLD

I don't want to hear about it.

MARIE-LOUISE

Sure, just one more thing for me to deal with
myself. You'd like that, wouldn't you, to spend your
life and not have a clue what goes on around you,
eh Léopold?

MANON

I don't care what you say ... It's like water off a
duck's back.

CARMEN

That's exactly your problem, kiddo, nothing
touches you. Only stuff that happened ten, fifteen
years ago. The only reason to live now is so you can
suffer real good so you can go fling yourself at the
feet of Jesus. Hey, come to think of it, there's a man
for you ...

MANON

Watch out, you're going too far.

CARMEN

Mind you, he's not exactly dangerous.

MARIE-LOUISE

I'm supposed to have supper ready, the kids lined
up like soldiers and me standing attention by the
stove when you walk in here at night. And when
supper's over it's your living room, your TV, your
beer, your chips. Then a nice big bed all to yourself
with no one to bother you the next morning when
you get sick. That way you can sail through life like
the King of England.

CARMEN

Last time I was here, you got me so depressed I
swore I'd never come back. Is your room still full of
holy pictures and statues, Manon?

MARIE-LOUISE

Well, sorry, Your Highness, there are times when
supper's late, the kids drive me nuts and I don't
have enough money to buy your lousy beer.

CARMEN

Do you know what year this is? You know, sometimes
I talk about you at the Rodéo, and they don't
believe me. They think I'm talking about my
mother! They can't believe my twenty-five-year-old
sister's so hung up on religion she is scared of her
own body ...

MARIE-LOUISE

So, you're the most miserable guy in the world:
everyone's out to get you. You see red and you start
swinging. No matter who, no matter how, makes no
difference to you: you get your revenge. And when
you've finished, you go to bed, fall asleep and
dream, in technicolour.

LEOPOLD

Shut your yap, you don't know what you're talking
about.

MARIE-LOUISE

If only that was true, if only I had no idea! No idea
of what I'm talking about. If only I was crazy!

CARMEN

Ten years later and you still try to act like Maman.
It's unbelievable! Right down to the candles and the
holy water!

MARIE-LOUISE

Now they must be happy, people who are crazy.

CARMEN
But you forget one thing. It's him you resemble,
with your one track mind.

MANON
That's not true.

CARMEN
You resemble him, him and his crazy family.

MARIE-LOUISE
Isn't that right Léopold? They must be really happy.
Eh, Léopold, I bet they're happy, the people who
are crazy.

LEOPOLD
Don't start on my family.

MARIE-LOUISE   *laughing*
I don't even have to mention their names. You
know right away who I mean. But I like to talk about
them.

CARMEN
Madness is hereditary, you know ...

MANON
If it is, you've got it, not me ...

CARMEN
Who's going nuts 'cause she lives in the past and
she hates a ghost? You or me?

MANON
Who's a whore on la rue St-Laurent?

CARMEN   *laughing*
I'm not a whore on la rue St-Laurent. I'm not a

whore at all. You sound like a nun, Manon. Whatever's beyond your doorstep, you don't understand and you don't want to understand, but you make sure you get it all wrong!

MARIE-LOUISE
Did you ever ask them if they're happy, Léopold? Eh? Did you ever ask them how they feel, inside?

LEOPOLD
I told you to shut up, Marie-Louise!

CARMEN
Anyway, I'd rather be a whore on la rue St-Laurent than an old maid playing with candles.

MARIE-LOUISE
You think they feel anything when they do their crazy stuff, Léopold? Eh? Eh? How about your father, when his eyes go all screwy and his tongue hangs out about three feet ... You ever ask him if he felt anything, inside?

LEOPOLD
Shut your mouth, Marie-Louise!

MARIE-LOUISE
You ought to find out, Léopold. After all, you might end up the same way. I mean, your father, your two sisters, your aunts, it wouldn't surprise me!

*LEOPOLD brings a beer bottle down
hard on the table.*

LEOPOLD
SHUT UP!

Long silence.

LEOPOLD

I don't want to hear any more about that stuff.

MANON

What do you expect me to do? Eh? Tell me, if you're so smart.

CARMEN

I already told you a hundred times ...

LEOPOLD

If only I could keep from thinking about it, too.

MANON

If I never had any friends, it's 'cause I'm too shy.

CARMEN

Shy! I don't call that shy! You'd almost scratch their eyes out if anyone came near you!

LEOPOLD

I don't want to become like them ...

CARMEN

You preferred to hide in here and spy on the rest of us.

MARIE-LOUISE

Well, when you see red and start having fits, you're their spitting image!

LEOPOLD

That's a lie! When I see red it's not fits. It's 'cause I've been drinking!

MARIE-LOUISE

That's how it starts ...

CARMEN
>You preferred to cling to Maman, to watch what she did ... To learn the right way to suffer like a true saint.

MARIE-LOUISE
>You know you're not supposed to drink! Not a drop!

CARMEN
>You've kept all her religious crap and you carry on just like her: washing and dusting them, polishing them up ... But since you're not Maman and Papa's not around to help you suffer the way you'd like, you sit here in the kitchen and run all those crazy scenes through your head. Isn't that right?

LEOPOLD
>I see red when I drink, but that doesn't mean I'm like them.

MARIE-LOUISE
>I keep telling you ...

LEOPOLD
>It's just that I can't help losing my temper ...

CARMEN
>If that's not crazy, I don't know what is. I can't walk in here, but I find you with a rosary in your hand. And within five minutes you start asking me, "Do you remember this, do you remember that." Of course I remember all that, Manon, and yes, it hurt me too. Of course I haven't forgotten! I was born in the shit just like you, Manon, but at least I try to get out. At least I try!

MANON
>By singing cowboy songs at the Rodéo!

48

CARMEN

Yeah, by singing cowboy songs at the Rodéo. For me, freedom means singing cowboy songs at the Rodéo. So what? It's better than being stuck in the past with a rosary in your hand and your eyes in the butter.

MARIE-LOUISE

You don't just lose your temper Léopold. You have real fits. Don't try to kid yourself ...

LEOPOLD

I see red and ...

MARIE-LOUISE

Crazy fits!

LEOPOLD

And ... It's true, after I can't remember ... It's true, I can't remember a thing ...

CARMEN

I've burned all the bridges, Manon ... Except one ...

MARIE-LOUISE

They're the same fits your father had just before he went completely bonkers. Do you remember how he did it, eh? Do you remember? What did the doctor tell him? The same thing he tells you: no alcohol! Not a drop. And what did you father do? Eh? Just what you're doing now: he drank like a fish. I know the phone number by heart, Léopold, and when your tongue starts hanging out and your eyes go screwy, believe me, it won't be long. Oh no, it won't be long. And I'll be rid of you, for good. And then peace! The holy peace! Jesus, will I have peace. Finally.

MANON
> Well, burn your last bridge and leave me in peace.

LEOPOLD
> I don't want to end up like that.

> *He drinks.*

> I think about it all the time ... It runs in the family ...
> Christ ... A whole family of screwballs ... My whole
> family, every one of them ... People like that
> shouldn't be allowed to have kids ... Maybe they
> shouldn't have let me have kids ...

> *He drinks.*

> I know I shouldn't drink ... but what else do I have,
> for Chrissake, what else do I have? I'm not about to
> go to the tavern and drink 7-Up! What would the
> others say ... Eh? My buddies ... My buddies ... My
> buddies.

MANON
> Maybe I'm happy the way I am ...

MARIE-LOUISE
> I'll sit alone in my corner of the living room, in
> front of the TV, the baby beside me ... and I'll knit
> ... I won't stop ... Till the day I die ... I'll just knit ...
> What glorious, heavenly peace! I'll be just fine.

MANON
> Maman used to say ...

LEOPOLD
> I've got no buddies ... I always sit in the corner,
> alone ... At an empty table ...

MANON

>Maman used to say, "If one day your father leaves, I'll stay here alone ... And I'll be happy ..."

LEOPOLD

>Not a one of those fuckers ever comes to sit with me ... Never! I don't go near them either, haven't for a long time ... It's been a long time since I tried to make friends with anyone ...

MARIE-LOUISE

>I'll be just fine.

LEOPOLD

>I got nothing to say to nobody ... nothing ...

MARIE-LOUISE

>I'll just sit in my corner ... And knit ...

LEOPOLD

>I sit down at an empty table ... I tell the waiter to set it up ... And I empty it ... When I've finished, when I've emptied them all, there's a kind of thick haze around the table and everyone else disappears. I'm all alone in the tavern! And I'm just fine! I don't hear a thing ... I don't see a thing ... I'm all alone in my haze. What peace! ... I close my eyes ... And everything's turning ... It's great ... I yell "Waiter" and when I open my eyes, the table's full! I say just the word, one word, and the table's full! But I don't drink. Not this time! Never the second time! I don't even touch them ... I just look at them. They're all there in front of me. The whole table, covered with beers. Mine. All mine. My table and my beer. If I don't want to touch 'em, fine ... If I do want to ... That's what it is to be rich.

MARIE-LOUISE

People will come to call and I'll say, "My husband? Oh, he's in the asylum ... He's crazy, you know. We had to put him away, he was uncontrollable ... Oh, the things he did ... Why, I remember ..." And I'll tell them all sorts of stories ... while I knit ... I'll tell them stories about you, Léopold, some true, some not true ... And they'll feel sorry for me. I'll be able to knit in peace and I'll know that at least people will feel sorry for me ... Léopold ... Léopold?

LEOPOLD

What?

MARIE-LOUISE

I can't wait for you to be really crazy.

CARMEN

She always wished he'd die. Poor Maman!

MANON

No, she didn't want him to die ... I know what she wanted.

MARIE-LOUISE   *laughing*

The look on your face! You should see the look on your face! You know it's true, don't you?

LEOPOLD   *smiling*

Sure, I know.

MARIE-LOUISE

Don't try to pretend, Léopold; don't try to smile, I know you're furious. You're trying to control yourself aren't you? I'm needling you, and you're trying not to blow your stack ...

MANON
    I know what she wanted ...

LEOPOLD
    And if I feel like it, I can knock over the table and
    spill the beer 'cause it's mine, 'cause I paid for it, so
    I can do what I like with it. And most of the time,
    that's just what I do. I lean back in my chair, put my
    foot on the edge of the table, and ...

    The lights change suddenly.

    MARIE-LOUISE screams.

MARIE-LOUISE
    You crazy bastard. What are you doing? You've
    knocked over the table!

MANON
    Carmen, did you hear? We've got to go.

CARMEN
    You stay here.

MARIE-LOUISE
    Carmen! Manon! Help me!

MANON
    We've got to go!

MARIE-LOUISE
    Quick! Help me!

MANON
    We've got to go!

MARIE-LOUISE
    Quick! Help me!

MANON
> She's calling us!

MARIE-LOUISE
> Your father's having another fit!

CARMEN
> You want to watch, eh?

MARIE-LOUISE
> Help! The bastard's going to kill me!

CARMEN
> You just want to see them fight.

MARIE-LOUISE
> He's going to kill me!

CARMEN
> Okay, come on, we'll see!

LEOPOLD   *slowly*
> And then, the haze disappears ...

MARIE-LOUISE
> Don't be afraid ...

LEOPOLD
> ... somebody grabs me ...

MARIE-LOUISE
> He doesn't see us ...

MANON   *very slowly*
> Did he hurt you, Maman?

MARIE-LOUISE
> No, he didn't touch me ...

CARMEN   *very slowly*
>   Then why did you say he was going to kill you?

LEOPOLD
>   ... And they throw me out ...

MARIE-LOUISE
>   Carmen, don't stand in the doorway. Come and
>   help us.

LEOPOLD
>   I find myself on the street ... My mouth full of blood
>   ...

MARIE-LOUISE
>   Manon, pick up the tablecloth and the dishes.

LEOPOLD
>   My mouth's full of blood ...

MARIE-LOUISE
>   Come on, help me lift the table.

LEOPOLD
>   And then ... Everything turns red. All I can see is
>   red. I could take the whole world in my hands and
>   crush it.

>   *Very long silence.*

MARIE-LOUISE
>   Go on now, get out of here. Both of you, go on, get
>   out, he's okay now ... I don't think he even noticed
>   ... I'll put a coldpack on his forehead.

CARMEN
>   She said he was gonna kill her ... but he was sitting
>   in his chair ... He didn't budge ... Bloody liar!

MANON

He's crazy, Carmen, really crazy!

CARMEN

That must make you both real happy.

The lights return to normal.

MARIE-LOUISE

Here, put this on your forehead ... you feel better?
... Can you hear me?

LEOPOLD

Yeah, yeah, I hear you ...

MARIE-LOUISE

You know what you did?

LEOPOLD   *laughing*

Yeah, I knocked over the peanut butter.

MANON

When I wake up in the morning I always think I'm
gonna hear them yelling ... For a moment it's like
I'm a child again, back in our old room. I'm sure
Maman's gonna scream ... Then, when I open my
eyes ...

CARMEN

You're disappointed ...

MARIE-LOUISE

That's the first time it's happened like this, before
breakfast. If you're gonna start smashing things
when you haven't even been drinking ...

LEOPOLD

You'd like me to smash everything in the house,
wouldn't you, once and for all?

CARMEN

So you take Maman's rosary, you kneel at Maman's side of the bed and you say Maman's prayers.

MANON

I don't even look at his side ... I'm afraid he might be there.

LEOPOLD

You'd love that, wouldn't you, to have to put me away?

CARMEN

You'd love that, wouldn't you, for him to really be there?

LEOPOLD

Well, you got a long wait ahead of you, you bitch. Don't count on it too fast, your quiet little old age, all to yourself, Marie-Louise ... my sweetheart ... my pretty little Marie-Lou ...

CARMEN

You'd love to have him laugh at you and yank that rosary out of your hands, just like he did with her ...

LEOPOLD

Hey! Hey, you remember that? Remember, Marie-Louise, when I used to call you "Marie-Lou"?

MANON

Maman was so devout ... She couldn't stand it when he insulted the Church ...

MARIE-LOUISE

Do I remember! Everytime you do something stupid you end up talking about when you used to call me "Marie-Lou"! ... That was a long time ago, Léopold ... a long time.

57

CARMEN

You poor fool! Have you never realized that Maman used religion the same way you do?

LEOPOLD

But you haven't forgotten ...

MARIE-LOUISE

You remind me often enough, whining like a baby and begging forgiveness, how can I forget?

CARMEN

Maman was no more religious than I am Manon. All that stuff was just a front. She hid behind it to get more pity.

MANON

How can you talk about her that way?

LEOPOLD

Those were the good times ...

MANON

I don't know what you mean.

MARIE-LOUISE

Oh, Christ almighty, were they the good times!

CARMEN

You know bloody well what I mean. Don't be such a hypocrite!

LEOPOLD

What? It's not true?

MARIE-LOUISE

Sure it's true, they were great ...

CARMEN

She was a screwed-up woman who flung herself on
religion like it was candy. She worked out her
frustrations on church railings but she never gave a
thought to what she was doing. She threw herself on
her knees so she wouldn't have to go to bed.

MARIE-LOUISE

Those were the days of peppermints and sugar
candy, chocolate honeymoons, caramel sundaes ...
A past like that sticks to you for a long time.

MANON

That's not true. I'd see her praying beside the bed
for a whole afternoon.

CARMEN

But do you know what was going through her head?
What do you think of when you kneel down beside
the bed? Do you think of God with His angels and
saints? No way! You imagine you're your mother
and your father's going to come along and snatch
your pretty rosary ... And you love it! That's got
nothing to do with religion ...

MARIE-LOUISE

Last week when I was cleaning out your bottom
drawer I found an old photograph. It must have
been taken some time in the forties ... I don't know
if you know the one I mean ... It's a picture my
mother took of me and my three sisters ...

LEOPOLD

Yeah, I remember ... You're wearing slacks, I think,
all four of you, and across the bottom you'd written,
"Forever Yours, Marie-Lou" ... "Forever Yours."

MARIE-LOUISE
    ... "Forever" ... "Forever." Boy, if I'd ever known ...

MANON
    You've no idea what you're talking about, Carmen
    ...

LEOPOLD
    You're not the only one who regrets it, you know? If
    I'd known I wouldn't have married you either.
    Maybe I'd be a happy man today. In the army ... or
    in prison ... Anywhere but here, but somewhere
    else, goddamn it! Somewhere else!

MARIE-LOUISE
    That's it, start shouting again and you'll have
    another fit!

MANON
    When you've been kneeling for a long time,
    concentrating with all your strength, you get so
    you're all dizzy, as if everything expands inside your
    head! Everything gets bigger. Sometimes it makes
    me shiver, Carmen ... It's true ... I shake like a leaf, I
    lose my balance ... It's incredible ... It's like ... it's
    like I'm floating! I get up, I come in here to sit, I
    rock for a while, and then I start again. I lean my
    head on the back of the chair ... You can't imagine
    ...

MARIE-LOUISE
    Won't this be a happy household when the new
    baby arrives. Already, with Roger you pretty near
    killed him when he cried at night ... What'll it be
    like with this one ...

LEOPOLD
    You should hear yourself, the way you tell things ...
    You exaggerate so much, you're funny ...

CARMEN
But what do you think about to get you going like that? That's what counts.

MARIE-LOUISE
I don't exaggerate.

CARMEN
You'd never admit what you think about, to get off on your balloon like that. But I know damn well it isn't God.

LEOPOLD
She doesn't exaggerate! When did I almost kill Roger because I couldn't sleep? Maybe I said I'd kill him if he didn't shut up, but I never touched him!

MARIE-LOUISE
Not when he was small ... You let him grow a bit first ... Now you like to beat the shit out of him!

CARMEN
When you saw Maman pray it was because she wanted you to. And when you're praying you always hope someone'll come in and discover you ... Maybe someone like Papa ...

LEOPOLD
Sure, on top of everything, I beat my kids ...

MARIE-LOUISE
You're not a child-beater, Léopold, you're just ...

LEOPOLD
"Just" what.

MARIE-LOUISE
I don't know ...

MANON
>Papa will hardly "discover" me. He's been dead for
>ten years.

CARMEN
>Not in your head ...

MARIE-LOUISE
>You're just a guy who's screwed up his whole life
>and who takes it out on his family instead of himself
>...

LEOPOLD
>You sure know how to simplify things.

MANON
>And I pray for him ... because ... he might be in Hell
>...

LEOPOLD
>You want to know what you are, Marie-Louise?

CARMEN
>If you really are praying, Manon, it's to keep him
>there, not to get him out.

MARIE-LOUISE
>This should be good. Make it short.

MANON
>You don't get out of Hell ...

LEOPOLD
>You're a frustrated old maid, that's what. Short
>enough for you?

CARMEN
>Then why pray?

MARIE-LOUISE
    It's short enough, but it doesn't mean anything.

MANON
    You can never be sure if someone's there or not ...

LEOPOLD
    Like hell! It means everything ...

CARMEN
    So why do you pray, with your eyes in the butter?

MARIE-LOUISE
    Sure, I mean I never should have gotten married,
    the whole world knows, that ...

LEOPOLD
    But not everybody knows why!

MARIE-LOUISE
    And you do ...

LEOPOLD
    You're damn right I do ...

MARIE-LOUISE   *laughing*
    All right, let's hear it ...

MANON
    Carmen, Papa killed himself, and he killed Maman
    and Roger ...

CARMEN
    Will you stop that! Stop twisting everything around.
    You're the one who decided he killed himself. You
    dreamed it up in your stupid little head and you
    won't let go.

MANON

It's true, Carmen, I know it's true. I heard them, that Saturday morning.

CARMEN

You always come back to that! It was ten years ago! Imagine how much you've invented since ...

MANON

I've invented nothing!

CARMEN

When you take off on your balloons, don't you add a little on? Then don't you keep what you've added and invent a bit more? I was here too, that Saturday morning; I heard them too. But whenever you tell the story, there's something you always leave out ... They said a lot of things you don't want to remember ... You tell it as if Maman's the only one to be pitied, but you forget that Papa ...

MANON

Papa never deserved pity!

CARMEN

He deserved as much as she did, Manon. Don't you remember what we heard when you dragged me down the hall because you were too scared to go by yourself?

MANON

Yes, I remember ... But it's Papa who was in the wrong ...

LEOPOLD

You can laugh all you want, say I'm a bastard, a failure, I'm crazy, anything you want ... But I've got just one word, just one word that'll shut you up fast ...

MANON

You always come back to that, too ... As if there was nothing else to life ...

CARMEN

Of course, there's more to life than that, Manon, but it sure makes things more livable.

MARIE-LOUISE

Come on, let's hear it, your word ...

LEOPOLD

Even in front of the kids, since all three of them are hiding behind the door?

The lights change.

CARMEN

He knows we're here ... Come on ...

MARIE-LOUISE

I've nothing to hide from my kids. I'll have them come in if you like ...

MANON

No, stay here.

LEOPOLD

Okay, go on. Call them in.

CARMEN

You really want a beating, don't you? You're just begging for it ...

MARIE-LOUISE

I'd rather not, you'll say something filthy just to get me mad ... You're crazy enough ...

LEOPOLD
    Scared, aren't you? ...

MARIE-LOUISE
    Not for myself ...

LEOPOLD
    Oh yes, you are!

MARIE-LOUISE
    Not in the least!

LEOPOLD
    ... and a lot more than you are for the kids. You've
    already started talking about filth, Marie-Louise ...
    You guessed it right off ...

MARIE-LOUISE
    So I was right ... It's that again ... That's all you ever
    think about ...

MANON
    Carmen, I'm getting out of here ...

    CARMEN bursts out laughing.

LEOPOLD
    You got it, it's that again ... Now get this, you nosey
    brats ... You too, Carmen, you think it's so funny ...
    Your mother here's got a problem. She's always had
    it and she always will: it's her cunt.

    CARMEN stops laughing.

MARIE-LOUISE
    Léopold! Roger's too young for that!

MANON

Carmen, I don't want to hear this, I don't want to
hear.

CARMEN

You wanted to come, now stay here and listen!

LEOPOLD

No, Roger's not too young to hear this! Kids today
know more than we do, for Chrissake. You're the
one who's a baby, Marie-Louise. Anyway, it's time
our kids found out! It's time they stopped taking me
for a monster and a bastard because you scream
bloody murder everytime I come near you ...

MARIE-LOUISE

Shut your mouth!

LEOPOLD

I'm not ashamed of what I've got to say, Marie-
Louise!

MARIE-LOUISE

Then fine, go ahead and say it! Just say it! Say it, so
once and for all we'll all know what bothers you so
much! Say it, and maybe then I'll know what comes
over you when you throw yourself at me like an
animal ...

LEOPOLD

You see, you put me down before I even start!
There's one thing you've never understood Marie-
Louise ... When I try to come near you in bed ...
When I ask you nicely why you don't want me to
touch you ... And you know, you know I've tried to
do that gently ... Marie-Louise, I don't have the
words for this this ...

MARIE-LOUISE
>So shut your mouth, you filthy pig!

>>*LEOPOLD brings his fist down on the table.*

LEOPOLD
>If I have to shout to make you understand, then I'll shout goddamn it. If you hadn't been so scared of your cunt, your whole fuckin' life, if you'd have let yourself go once in a while, just a little, things might be a lot better in this house, Marie-Louise!

MARIE-LOUISE
>Léopold!

LEOPOLD
>If you wouldn't act like an old maid who keeps her cherry in the fridge, if you'd just enjoy it, a bit, a good screw, then we might be able to stand it around here.

MARIE-LOUISE
>Will you shut up! Will you shut up in front of the kids, you pig!

LEOPOLD
>Hah? I told you I could shut your big yap with just one word! It's true what you said a while ago: In twenty years of marriage I've only had you four times. That's the four times I got you pregnant. But that doesn't make me a bastard. You think it's normal? You think it's normal for married people to do it four times in twenty years?

MARIE-LOUISE
>You'd have us do it four times a day, like animals. You expect me to act like the whores on the Main?

LEOPOLD   *softly*
> Why not?

MARIE-LOUISE
> You're crazy ... You really are crazy!

LEOPOLD
> It's not me who's crazy, Marie-Louise ... If you
> hadn't been so fucked up, you and your sisters ...
> and your mother ...

MARIE-LOUISE
> My mother had fourteen kids, and I didn't want
> that for me ...

LEOPOLD
> She could have had forty kids, that doesn't mean
> she liked it ... It doesn't mean her and your old man
> did it for pleasure ... But who knows, maybe she
> wasn't as screwed up as you ...

MARIE-LOUISE
> For pleasure ...

LEOPOLD
> Yes, pleasure, Marie-Louise, pleasure. Believe it or
> not, you don't get married just to have kids! And if
> you absolutely have to talk about God, 'cause I see
> you coming with your shit about Him ... Well, your
> bloody God put pleasure into it, and he didn't do it
> for nothing!

MARIE-LOUISE
> Leave God out of this Léopold! You don't know
> what you're saying! Maybe God did put pleasure
> into it, but it's only there for the man.

LEOPOLD
        Women can come too!

MARIE-LOUISE
        I'm not a pig, Léopold!

LEOPOLD
        Jesus Christ, are you thick! I'm not asking you to be
        a pig!

MARIE-LOUISE
        Yes you are! For me, to do that is to be a pig! It's for
        animals. I will never do that with pleasure, Léopold,
        never! Never!

        The lights return to normal.

CARMEN
        You ran back to our room, you closed the door and
        you hid under the covers. You knew he was right ...
        For once, I stayed behind the door ... And I swore to
        myself ...

LEOPOLD
        There aren't many people like us left, Marie-Louise,
        and thank God for that ...

MANON
        If you swore to make your husband happy, you sure
        missed the boat!

MARIE-LOUISE
        You think they're happier, people who start doing
        that at fourteen or fifteen!

MANON
        The way you're going now, you'll never even find a
        husband.

70

LEOPOLD
> Yes, I think they're happier ...

CARMEN
> Don't worry, I never swore I'd make any man happy
> ... I like my independence too much.

LEOPOLD
> If you hadn't always been so closed up, you think
> we'd be fighting like this, this morning?

CARMEN
> I only swore I'd get out of this rat trap sooner, that's
> all ...

MARIE-LOUISE
> No, I suppose we'd still be in bed.

CARMEN
> That I'd get away from here ...

MARIE-LOUISE
> I'd rather fight, Léopold ...

CARMEN
> Far away ...

LEOPOLD
> You can't even talk about it ... much less do it ...

MANON
> You never got past the Main ...

CARMEN
> Manon, you can stay in your living room and still
> get far away from something that's dragging you
> down. You just have to break with whatever it is
> that's put you in the shit!

MARIE-LOUISE
    I might have been able to do it, Léopold, if ...

LEOPOLD
    If what?

MANON
    So the day they died, you already wanted to leave ...

CARMEN
    That Saturday morning I realized the same thing as
    Papa ... That they would forever be stuck in their
    shit ... And I decided that at least I would get out ...

MARIE-LOUISE
    I might have been able to do it, and maybe, maybe I
    could have enjoyed it, if *you'd* known how, Léopold!

CARMEN
    I knew they'd go on blaming each other for the rest
    of their lives. Without ever realizing it was both
    their faults. Not just Papa's, Manon ...

MARIE-LOUISE
    You don't answer ... I've got you now, don't I? If
    only you knew how to go about it. You think what
    you do to me is pleasant for a woman?

CARMEN
    They spent twenty years of their lives fighting, and if
    they'd lived another twenty, they'd have gone on
    fighting ... Until they dropped! Because they
    couldn't touch one another without thinking that
    one wanted to hurt the other ...

MARIE-LOUISE
    My mother said to me, "I don't know if he's a boy
    for you, I don't know ... He's got funny eyes. Back

72

home in the country I wouldn't let you marry him, but here in the city you've met lots, I suppose you know what you want ..."

Silence.

"I suppose you know what you want." ... Oh, it's true, I knew what I wanted all right; to get out of the house as fast as I could. There were so many people in that house and we were so poor ... I was ashamed! I wanted out, to breathe a little. It's true, I met lots of boys. But him, he was nicer than the others and I thought he'd just change houses for me and the new one wouldn't be so crowded ... It'd be cleaner, quieter ... I hardly knew I had to let my husband do with me as he pleased ... My mother ... I'll never, ever, forgive her for not telling me more ... All my mother said was, "When your husband comes near you, close your eyes and go stiff as a board. You have to put up with it all ... It's your duty." Well, I did my duty, goddamn it! And you bastard ... You hurt me! Oh, how you hurt me. I wanted to scream, but my mother told me to grit my teeth. And you, you had no idea ... You were pissed to the gills because you were embarrassed and you couldn't even control yourself ... Well, you got unembarrassed soon enough. I said to myself, "If that's what sex is, then never again. Never! Never!" When you'd had your fun, you rolled over with a burp and fell asleep like a baby. It was the first time a man ever slept beside me. He turned his back, he snored and he stunk! I could have died right then and there! When you got up the next morning you talked about it like it was some sort of bingo game, making your stupid jokes ... You ignorant bastard! It's not true, you know. Not once, not once have you ever tried to be gentle ... You're gentle

73

beforehand, when you lie there begging for it, but two seconds later you're like a raging bull! If you had known how to go about it, then maybe ... just maybe ... But I'm too old to regret all that now ...

CARMEN

What can you expect in a house where people scream bloody murder if anyone even touches somebody else?

MANON

You must be happy now, you can touch all the people you like.

CARMEN

Yes, I can touch whoever I like ... And I don't look like a corpse, either!

MARIE-LOUISE

You're always full of beer and you stink when you come near me, Léopold. You've got bad breath. I'm a human being too, you know. You say women can enjoy it ... But have you ever tried, just once, just once in your life, to ...

LEOPOLD

You're not a pig but you're plenty screwed up, aren't you, Marie-Louise? You're not a pig but you wish you could be, eh, my pretty Marie-Lou? But you don't know how. I get my kicks, you can get yours.

MARIE-LOUISE stops knitting. She puts down her knitting.

MANON

If you've found your happiness, leave me in peace ... I've found my own ...

CARMEN
> Your happiness stinks, Manon. It stinks of death.
> For ten years you've reeked of it. They're dead, and
> it's a good thing they are, Manon.

MARIE-LOUISE
> "I get my kicks, you can get yours!" I was reading in
> the *Digest* the other day that a family is like a living
> cell, that each member's supposed to contribute to
> the life of that cell ... Cell, my ass! It's a cell all right,
> but not that kind. When people like us get married,
> it's to be all alone, together. You're all alone, your
> husband's alone beside you, and your kids are alone
> all around you. And we all look at one another like
> cats and dogs. A gang of people who are all alone,
> together, that's what we are!
>
> > *She laughs.*
>
> And when you're young, you dream of getting out,
> of finding some place where you can breathe ...
> Christ! So you leave ... And you find another cell of
> people alone, together ... "I get my kicks, you can
> get yours!" Shit!
>
> > *She laughs.*

LEOPOLD
> What's so funny all of a sudden?

MARIE-LOUISE
> I'm getting my kicks, my love ...

CARMEN
> The deeper you sink into your worst memories, the
> happier you are ...

MARIE-LOUISE
> And when you look around, you realize it's the same
> story everywhere ... Your brother, your sisters, who
> all married for love, what do they look like after
> twenty years? Corpses.

CARMEN
> You look like a corpse, Manon.

LEOPOLD
> You know what I feel like doing sometimes, my
> precious Marie-Lou? I'd like to take the car, get you
> and Roger in it, drive out on the parkway and smash
> the mother into a concrete wall ... Carmen and
> Manon are big enough to look out for themselves ...
> But the rest of us ... We're of no use ... to anybody ...

CARMEN
> When I went out that door right after the accident,
> I took a deep breath and I told myself, the time for
> tears is over, Carmen. Finished. Forget everything,
> and start all over, as if nothing has happened.

LEOPOLD
> We're like little gears in a big machine ... And we're
> afraid to fight back 'cause we think we're too small
> ...

CARMEN
> And I managed to get rid of my past, for a while ...
> A big hole in my brain ... I didn't want to know
> about them ... That's how I managed to do what I
> wanted. I never dared tell anyone I wanted to sing
> but after that I was free to go out and do it. I kept
> telling myself, the time for tears is over ... So move. I
> won't say it wasn't tough, 'cause it was ... But I never
> complained.

76

LEOPOLD

But if a gear gets busted, the machine might jam ...
you never know ...

CARMEN

Some people think it's dumb, a girl who sings
cowboy songs ... But if that's what you want to do,
and you manage to do it, you're not half as dumb as
they are. You don't care if you starve for a while
because you know that at least you like what you're
doing ... I like what I do Manon ...

LEOPOLD

You never know, the machine might jam ...

CARMEN

But you never understood any of that ... You've just
wallowed in tears instead of trying to get out.

LEOPOLD

It's one hell of a big machine ...

CARMEN

You've got to understand, it's time to throw your
rosary on the floor, dump your plaster saints in the
garbage, put the key in the door, and leave all this
crap behind you. Fight back, Manon, it's all you've
got left!

MARIE-LOUISE

It's not true I don't want this baby ...

CARMEN

Empty your mind! Throw your memories away! Put
an end to this slavery! Don't sit here doing nothing.
DO SOMETHING!

MANON

No, I can't. It's too late ...

CARMEN

I'll help you.

MANON

No. You disgust me! You're filthy!

MARIE-LOUISE

It's not true I don't want this baby ... I want it. Oh
yes, I want it! With the others, I couldn't take care
of them because I was too ignorant. I didn't know
how, or I was too busy ... But this one ... I'm going to
love this one ... It's the one I'll have really loved ...
Oh how I'll love it ... And no one's gonna touch it ...
It'll be my baby ... I'll bring it up ... And I won't let
anyone near it ... It'll be my baby ... All mine ... At
last I'll be able to love someone.

CARMEN

You're the one who's filthy, Manon.

MARIE-LOUISE

Him, he won't touch it ... I'll never let him put his
filthy hands on this one.

CARMEN   *very slowly*

Me? ... I'm free. You hear me? Free! When I climb
up on that stage at night and step in front of the
mike, the music starts and I tell myself, if they
weren't dead I probably wouldn't be here ... And
when I start my first cowboy song, I'm so glad
they're dead.

MANON

Get out!

CARMEN
>And I'm so glad to be free of all the shit that went
>on in this prison ... The men in the audience, they
>look at me ... They're never the same, they change
>every night, but every night, they're mine!

MANON
>Get out!

CARMEN
>I think ... I'm a good singer, Manon!

MANON
>Get out!

CARMEN
>And ... I'm ... happy.

MANON
>Get out!

>>*CARMEN gets up to leave.*

CARMEN
>You'll end up like them, Manon. You hear me? But I
>won't feel sorry for you. No matter how hard you
>try! You're not pitiable, Manon. When I walk out
>that door, I'm going to forget you ... You too!

>>*She leaves.*

>>*MANON falls to her knees.*

MANON
>Thank you, Dear God ...

MARIE-LOUISE   *looking at LEOPOLD for the first time*
>Léopold.

MANON
    Thank you, dear God ... Thank you ... Thank you.

LEOPOLD
    What ...

MARIE-LOUISE
    You'll never know how much I hate you.

LEOPOLD   *getting up*
    You want to go for a ride with me in the car tonight,
    Marie-Lou?

        *After a long silence, MARIE-LOU gets
        up.*

        BLACK.